WHERE IS THE TOP OF THE WORLD?

...and more about planet Earth

CHRYSALIS CHILDREN'S BOOKS

First published in the UK in 2003 by
Chrysalis Children's Books PLC,
64 Brewery Road,
London N7 9NT

British Library Cataloguing in Publication Data for this book is available
from the British Library.

Every effort has been made to ensure that none of the recommended
websites in this book is linked to inappropriate material. However, due
to the nature of the Internet, the publishers regret that they cannot take
responsibility for future content of the websites.

Produced by Miles Kelly Publishing Ltd
Bardfield Centre, Great Bardfield, Essex CM7 4SL

Editorial Director: Anne Marshall
Editor: Mark Darling
Copy Editor: Sarah Ridley
Indexer: Jane Parker
Proofreader: Hayley Kerr, Leon Gray
Designer: Michelle Cannatella
Artwork Commissioning: Bethany Walker

Editorial Director, Chrysalis Children's Books: Honor Head

ISBN: 1 903954 91 6

Printed and bound in Malaysia

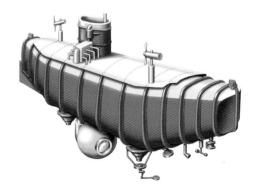

Contents

Why is our world so wet? 4

Why is the Earth crusty? 4

Is the world cracking up? 5

What makes the Earth like a meteorite? 5

Were rocks always cool and hard? 6

Why are some rocks always left behind? 7

How does rock get its marbles? 7

Where is the top of the world? 8

How can a mountain fold up? 9

Why are some peaks all white? 9

How does a mountain blow its top? 10

Where would you find a ring of fire? 11

How can volcanoes sleep? 11

Why does the ground get steamed up? 11

What makes the ground shiver? 12

Can dogs hear earthquakes coming? 13

Why should you run from a tsunami? 13

Why does water go round and round? 14

What is the world's longest river? 15

What makes a river roar? 15

Why is the world's biggest desert full of water? 16

How is ice like a river? 17

When is ice 'fast'? 17

When does the sea have a break? 18

When does the sea find the Moon attractive? 19

Why make groynes? 19

What's the point of coastlines? 19

Can we touch the sea's bottom? 20

How do you hear the sea bed? 20

Are there mountains under the sea? 21

Why are clouds fluffy or flat? 22

Why did the thunder clap? 22

Why are some clouds like horses' tails? 23

When does wind twist? 24

When does it rain blood? 24

Which winds have eyes? 25

Why is the desert deserted? 26

Why is the ground crazy? 27

Where's the world's biggest sandpit? 27

What rocks hang tight? 28

What are the world's biggest holes? 29

What makes rocks dissolve? 29

Why are rainforests vanishing? 30

Why is the taiga green? 31

Where do trees undress for winter? 31

Index 32

Make-its

Make your own sedimentary rock 7

Make an erupting volcano 11

Make your own river 15

Make your own lightning 23

Making stalactites 29

Why is our world so wet?

Seen from space, our world stands out as a blue planet. This is because much of it is covered by water. Our world is special because without water there can be no life. Mars is the only other planet with water, although all of this is frozen. The Earth has loads of water because billions of years ago it was hit by giant snowballs from space called comets. The snow melted to form the oceans.

↓ Why is the Earth crusty?

The Earth is made mostly of rock, but it is not just a giant pebble. In fact, it is more like an egg. It has a thin shell of hard rock called the crust. Under the crust there is a mantle of softer rock, like the egg white. And right in the centre is the yolk, or core, of the Earth, which is liquid.

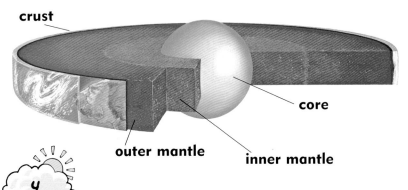

crust

core

outer mantle

inner mantle

4

INTERNET LINK

Discover records about Earth
http://extremescience.com/earthsciport.htm

Find out more about plate tectonics
www.brainpop.com/science/earth

⬇ Is the world cracking up?

The Earth's shell or crust is not as smooth and solid as it looks. Actually, it is cracked into 15 or so slabs of rock – almost like the cracked shell of a hard-boiled egg. These slabs are called tectonic plates. These plates have been moving very slowly for millions of years.

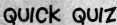

QUICK QUIZ

1. How long does it take the Earth to turn round once?
2. What is the largest ocean in the world called?
3. Name the two planets closest to Earth?

....

Answers – see page 32.

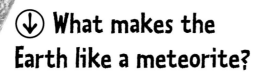

◀ *200 million years ago*

◀ *100 million years ago*

◀ *Today*

⬇ What makes the Earth like a meteorite?

Every now and then, the Earth is hit by rocks from space. These rocks are called meteorites. They are 4½ billion years old, exactly the same age as the Earth. And just like Earth, meteorites are made from rock and iron. In fact, the Earth is really a whole load of meteoroids squashed together.

Thick and crusty

- The Earth's crust is between 30 and 50 kilometres thick beneath land, but only 5 to 15 kilometres thick underneath the oceans.
- The Earth's plates move between 1 to 10 centimetres each year.
- Earth is 40,074 kilometres round the middle.
- Over 70% of the Earth's surface is covered by water!
- As Earth turns, places on the Equator are moving ½ kilometre every second!

5

Were rocks always cool and hard?

No. Some were once very hot indeed – and completely soft and runny. These rocks, called igneous rocks, came from deep inside the Earth where it is hot enough to melt rock into a liquid called magma. From time to time, magma bubbles up under the Earth's surface like hot sauce bubbling up under a pie crust. In places, it even bursts through a volcano as lava. Whenever it comes near the surface, magma eventually cools down and turns to solid rock.

▼ *It might look strange, but the 40,000 six-sided columns of the Giant's Causeway in Ireland formed naturally when volcanic lava cracked as it cooled.*

INTERNET LINK
Find out about rocks and how to collect them
http://www.fi.edu/fellows/payton/rocks/index2.html
Have some fun with games about rocks
http://www.surfnetkids.com/rocks.htm

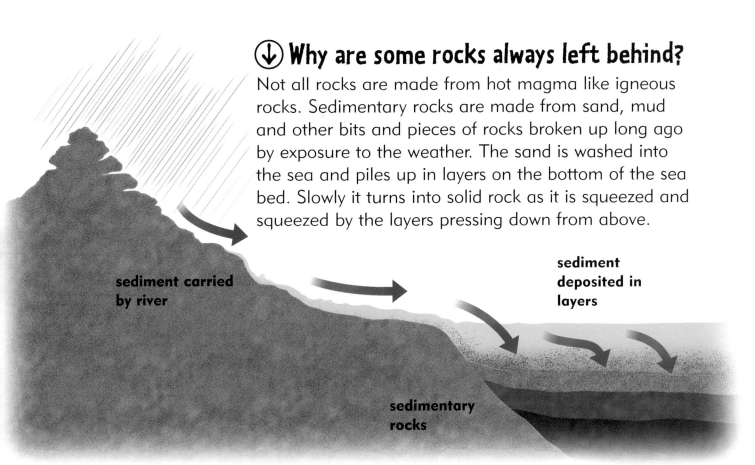

↓ Why are some rocks always left behind?

Not all rocks are made from hot magma like igneous rocks. Sedimentary rocks are made from sand, mud and other bits and pieces of rocks broken up long ago by exposure to the weather. The sand is washed into the sea and piles up in layers on the bottom of the sea bed. Slowly it turns into solid rock as it is squeezed and squeezed by the layers pressing down from above.

sediment carried by river

sediment deposited in layers

sedimentary rocks

↓ How does rock get its marbles?

Marble is a beautiful, shiny rock that sculptors and architects love. Sometimes it is pure sugar-white. Sometimes it is laced with colours like ripple ice cream. It is a special kind of rock called metamorphic rock. This means that it forms when another rock is heated by hot magma or when there is intense pressure on the rock. Marble forms when a rock called limestone is changed in this way.

Make your own sedimentary rock

You will need:
6 heaped tablespoons of wall filler, 3 cupfuls of sand, water and food colour, soft drinks bottle

1. Mix 2 heaped tablespoons of wall filler into about a cupful of sand, then add a little water, strongly coloured with food colour.

2. Make two more mixes in this way, adding different coloured water to each. Spoon them into the bottle in layers.

3. Turn the sand out of the bottle after a few days. Cut the bottle with scissors if necessary. The sand should now be hard rock in layers.

 # Where is the top of the world?

The highest places in the world are mountain tops or summits. Most high summits are in vast mountain ranges stretching for hundreds of kilometres. The world's highest mountain range is the Himalayas in southern Asia. Here, 14 summits rise over 8,000 metres above sea level, including Mount Everest.

▲ On 29 May 1953, Edmund Hillary of New Zealand and Tenzing Norgay of Nepal were the first human beings to reach the top of Mount Everest – the highest place on Earth.

INTERNET LINK

To learn more about the Rocky Mountains
www.americanparknetwork.com/parkinfo/rm

Got a tricky question about mountains?
http://walrus.wr.usgs.gov/docs/ask-a-ge.html/

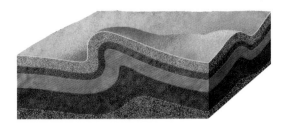

← How can a mountain fold up?

Apart from volcanoes, most rocks start off flat. So how do they rise up to form mountains? The answer is that they fold up like folds in a blanket. This happens when the tectonic plates, the giant slabs of rock that make up the Earth's crust, meet. These plates move about all the time. As one plate very slowly moves under the other, the rocks of the top plate are pushed upwards to form a mountain range.

High and mighty

- In 1999, satellite measurements showed Mount Everest was 2 metres taller than we thought, standing at 8,863 metres high.
- The Himalayas and Andes Mountains are actually growing taller all the time!
- The Chyulu Hills in Kenya make up the world's newest range of volcanic hills: one peak is less than 500 years old.
- The Appalachian Mountains may once have been as high as the Himalayas.

QUICK QUIZ
1. What is the highest mountain in North America?
2. What continent is Mount Everest in?
3. Is Mount Everest snow-capped?

....

Answers – see page 32.

↘ Why are some peaks all white?

Air gets colder the higher you go. Above a certain height, called the snow line, it can be so cold that snow never melts. This is why many mountains are capped in snow, even in summer. The height of the snow line varies dramatically between continents. Near the poles the snow line is at sea level!

▼ *Mountain tops are naturally cold, but high winds make the cold worse, which is why warm clothing is very important.*

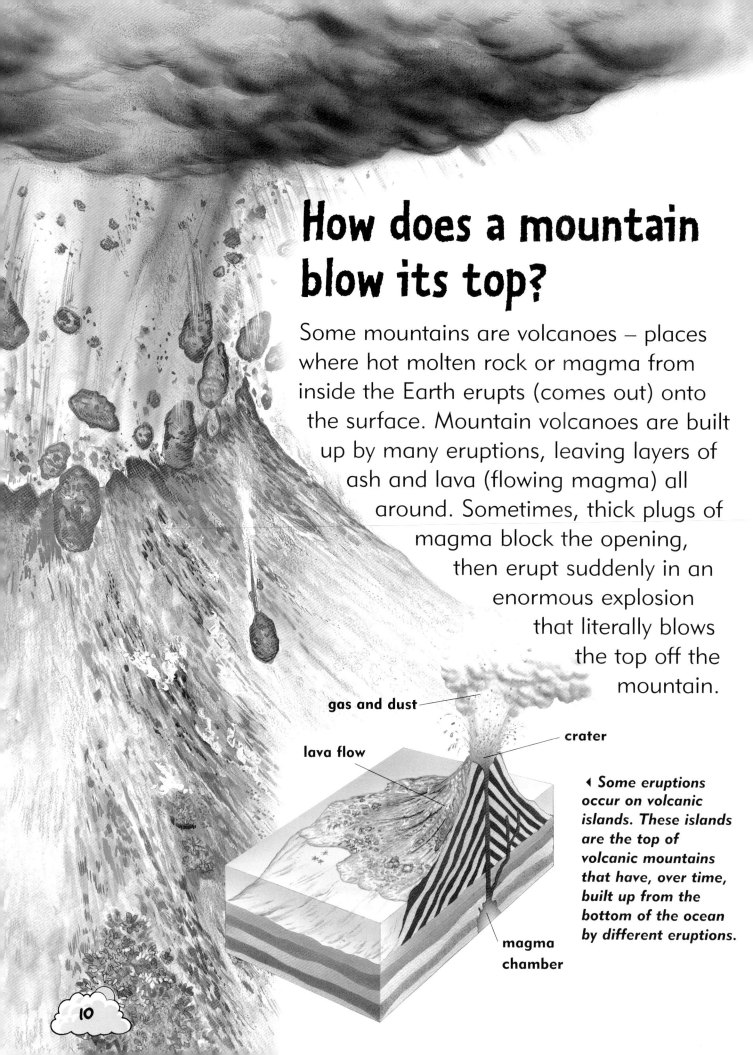

How does a mountain blow its top?

Some mountains are volcanoes – places where hot molten rock or magma from inside the Earth erupts (comes out) onto the surface. Mountain volcanoes are built up by many eruptions, leaving layers of ash and lava (flowing magma) all around. Sometimes, thick plugs of magma block the opening, then erupt suddenly in an enormous explosion that literally blows the top off the mountain.

gas and dust

lava flow

crater

◄ Some eruptions occur on volcanic islands. These islands are the top of volcanic mountains that have, over time, built up from the bottom of the ocean by different eruptions.

magma chamber

⊠ Where would you find a ring of fire?

Some parts of the world have more volcanoes than others. There are no volcanoes in the middle of Asia, for instance. But there are lots around the edge of the Pacific Ocean, including North America's Mount St. Helens. These volcanoes make up what is known as the Ring of Fire.

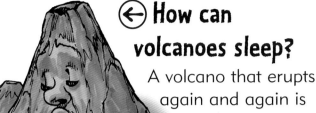

← How can volcanoes sleep?

A volcano that erupts again and again is called an active volcano. But no volcano goes on erupting forever. If it is quiet for some time – perhaps a century or more – scientists say it is dormant or sleeping. If it seems to stop erupting altogether, they say it is extinct.

⊠ Why does the ground get steamed up?

Rock and magma are able to stay hot underground long after a volcano stops erupting. If so, rain trickling into the ground can get incredibly hot. While it is trapped underground, the water cannot actually boil like a kettle, but it can bubble upwards. Then as soon as it reaches the surface, it is suddenly free to boil and sends up a huge whoosh of steam called a geyser.

Make an erupting volcano
You will need:
sand, marker pen, baking powder, red food colour, white vinegar

1. Make a small cone-shaped mountain with sand, then use a thick round marker pen to make a vent down the middle.

2. Carefully spoon a heaped tablespoon of baking powder into the vent of your volcano.

3. Add some red colouring to a quarter of a cupful of vinegar and quickly pour the mixture into the vent – then watch your volcano erupt!

INTERNET LINK
Find out about the biggest volcano eruptions
http://volcano.und.nodak.edu/vw.html
Simple volcano facts
http://www.fema.gov/kids/volcano.htm

What makes the ground shiver?

Even a passing train can make the ground tremble a little, but the ground really shivers violently when there is an earthquake. Earthquakes are usually started by tectonic plates moving. Tectonic plates are the huge slabs of rock that make up the Earth's surface. They move very slowly, and most of the time they slide past or under each other with no ill-effects. But every now and then they get jammed. Then pressure builds up so much that when they lurch on it causes a dramatic shudder, creating an earthquake.

▼ Earthquakes start when two segments of the Earth's surface move and jolt past or under each other.

INTERNET LINK

Fun quizzes and puzzles about earthquakes
http://www.abag.ca.gov/bayarea/eqmaps/kids.html

Learn more about earthquakes
http://www.fema.gov/kids/quake.htm

▼ A large earthquake can lay an entire city flat in just a few minutes.

← Can dogs hear earthquakes coming?

Many people think animals can sense earthquakes long before they arrive. Even before scientists detect faint vibrations, dogs are said to howl, pandas moan and mice scamper from their holes. No one knows if this is true or just folklore, but some scientists are studying animals to see if they might help us predict earthquakes.

On shaky ground

- In the 1989 San Francisco earthquake, collapsing freeways crushed some cars to just 0.5 metres thick.
- The worst earthquake in China in 1556 killed 830,000 people.
- The longest ever recorded earthquake in Alaska on 21 March 1964 lasted just four minutes.

QUICK QUIZ

1. The French capital Paris was completely destroyed by an earthquake in 1755: true or false?
2. In which year was San Francisco destroyed by an earthquake?
3. How fast can a tsunami travel at sea?

....

Answers – see page 32.

↓ Why should you run from a tsunami?

A tsunami (pronounced *soon-army*) is the world's most terrifying wave. It is started not by the wind, like ordinary waves, but by an earthquake under the sea. The earthquake sends a giant pulse of water racing along the seabed as fast as a jet plane. When this pulse reaches shallow water, it rears up in a giant wave tens of metres high that swamps any shore in its way.

Why does water go round and round?

The amount of water in the world always stays pretty much the same. Rainfall gathers in rivers, and rivers carry water down into the sea. But water evaporates off the sea and drifts up into the sky to make clouds – and the clouds give rain. So water is never lost. Instead it goes round forever, from rain to river, from river to sea, from sea to sky. This is called the water cycle.

▲ *Rivers wind from side to side in bends called meanders where they cross flatter ground.*

▼ *Water is not lost but goes round and round in a continuous cycle.*

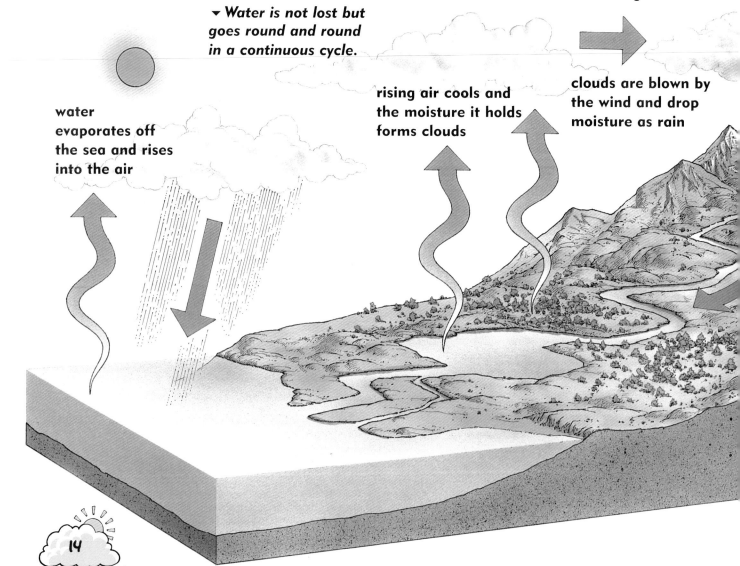

water evaporates off the sea and rises into the air

rising air cools and the moisture it holds forms clouds

clouds are blown by the wind and drop moisture as rain

→ What is the world's longest river?

The world's longest river is the Amazon in South America, which flows for 6,750 kilometres. Along most of its course the Amazon ranges from 2½ to 10 kilometres wide. It accounts for 20 per cent of the fresh water that flows into the world's oceans. So much water flows through the Amazon at its peak that it could flood the world's biggest sports stadium in 13 seconds!

rain falls on the land and gathers into rivers that run into the sea

↗ What makes a river roar?

Rivers roar where they flow over waterfalls – places where the river plunges straight down over a ledge. So much water flows over the Victoria Falls in Zimbabwe that its roar can be heard 16 kilometres away. Locals call the falls *Mosi oa Tunya*, the smoke that thunders. The huge Niagara Falls is one of the most famous sights in North America.

INTERNET LINK
Find out more about water on planet Earth
www.geography4kids.com/files/water_hydrosphere.html
Everything you need to know about water
http://ga.water.usgs.gov/edu/

Make your own river
You will need:
sand, large plastic tray, plastic bottle, hose

1. Fill the largest tray you can find with sand.

2. Smooth the sand as flat as you can, then set the tray up so that it slopes slightly.

3. Cut the bottle in half and press it firmly into the sand, as shown below.

4. Set the hose so that it trickles very slowly into the bottle and spills over.

5. Watch the stream of water run down the sand.

Over the next few hours see how meanders and branches develop in your stream.

# Why is the world's biggest desert full of water?

The world's biggest desert is Antarctica. It is a desert because it is far too cold here to rain. It doesn't even snow that much – the equivalent of less than 50 millimetres of rain a year (less than any desert). There is plenty of water here, though. In fact, Antarctica has 70 per cent of the world's fresh water. It is simply frozen into an ice sheet up to 5 kilometres thick.

▸ *Killer whales pounce on seals when they come up for air at the breathing holes they have made in the ice.*

▾ *The edge of the ice sheet advances and retreats with the seasons.*

INTERNET LINK

Fun with ice and snow
http://www.teelfamily.com/activities/snow/

Get the lowdown on glaciers
http://nsidc.org/glaciers/

➔ How is ice like a river?

In mountain regions it can be so cold that snow never melts. Over the years, unmelted snow may build up into a huge mass of solid ice. Eventually, the ice may become so heavy that it begins to flow downhill very slowly, like cold treacle. As the ice flows down through valleys, it forms rivers of slow flowing ice called glaciers. Glaciers creep down the valley until they melt in the warmer air below.

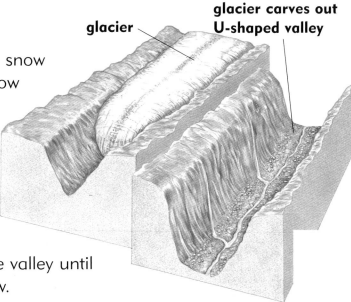
glacier
glacier carves out U-shaped valley

▲ Seals and whales are wrapped in thick layers of fat called blubber to keep them warm.

QUICK QUIZ
1. Does the Sun ever set at the South Pole?
2. Is it dark all through the winter at the North Pole?
3. Who led the first expedition to reach the South Pole?

....

Answers –
see page 32.

↗ When is ice 'fast'?

The Arctic is so cold that the sea here is mostly covered with a vast, floating ice sheet. The centre of this sheet, around the North Pole, is so cold that it never melts. This ice is called polar ice. Around the polar ice is pack ice, which melts a little and breaks up into chunks called floes in the summer. Fast ice forms in winter between pack ice and the land around the Arctic Ocean. It is called fast ice because it is held fast to the shore.

As cold as ice

● The biggest iceberg ever seen, in 1955, was 31,000 km², about the same size as Belgium.
● The ice in Arctic icebergs froze at the time the Egyptians were building the pyramids.
● Antarctic icebergs can be hundreds of kilometres long. In 2002, an ice sheet the size of New York State broke off.

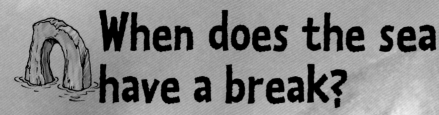

When does the sea have a break?

The sea breaks when waves crash upon the shore after travelling far across the ocean. When waves move, they pass across the sea like a package on a conveyor belt. The water in them barely moves forward at all, simply rolling around in a circle. Waves break on the shore when the water becomes so shallow that the water cannot roll right round in a circle. Instead, water at the top of the wave spills forward onto the shore, then falls back.

▸ *When waves move into shallow water they make the water rear up and crash down in surges of water called breakers.*

INTERNET LINK

Learn about the coast and its amazing wildlife
www.nationaltrust.org.uk/coastline/kids/

Find out how waves break and shape the shore
http://www.georesources.co.uk/leld.htm

sea cliffs

cave

stacks

arch

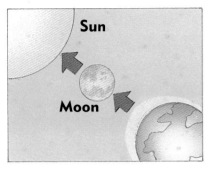

▲ *The highest tides occur when the Moon is in the right place for the Sun to add its gravitational pull.*

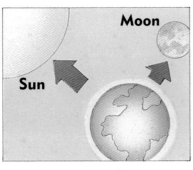

▲ *The gentlest tides occur when the Moon is in the place where the Sun's pull counteracts it.*

⬆ When does the sea find the Moon attractive?

Usually twice every day the sea rises and falls with the tides. Over the course of 12 hours or so the water rises a few metres, then drops back. Tides are caused by the pull of the Moon's gravity on the waters of the oceans as the Earth turns round. High tides occur in the places nearest to and futhest from the Moon. In between come low tides.

⬇ Why make groynes?

Sometimes, waves strike the beach at an angle and wash fine sand sideways. After a while all the fine sand is washed away, leaving only knobbly pebbles. So at some beaches, fences called groynes are built down the beach to hold on to the good sand.

estuary

beach

protective wall

groyne

⬆ What's the point of coastlines?

On sheltered coasts, waves wash sand into valleys and bays to create beaches. Yet on exposed coasts their constant pounding can wear away solid rock. The most exposed places are points or headlands sticking out into the sea, where waves crash with their full force. Here hills are undercut to create sheer cliffs and rocky stacks.

Can we touch the sea's bottom?

Oceans are quite shallow near coasts, but out in mid-ocean they are thousands of metres deep. The very deepest places are ocean trenches – deep valleys in the ocean floor. The deepest of all is the Mariana Trench in the Pacific Ocean, just over 11,000 metres deep. In 1960, the *Trieste*, a kind of underwater craft called a bathyscaphe, dived almost to the bottom here. Japanese engineers are working on a craft that may one day reach the very bottom.

⬇ How do you hear the sea bed?

We can't see the sea bed, but we can make maps of it using sound. Special sonar machines send out a pulse of sound that bounces off the sea bed, then is picked up by the sonar again. The time the sound takes to bounce back shows exactly how far down the sea bed is.

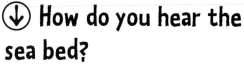

⬇ Are there mountains under the sea?

Much of the deep ocean floor is a wide plain covered in slime. But here and there are giant mountains thousands of metres high. A few seamounts are so high they poke up above the surface, forming islands. Most, though, are completely submerged. Flat-topped seamounts may be old volcanoes that once projected above the surface.

QUICK QUIZ

1. The world has four great oceans: Pacific, Indian, Arctic and ... what?
2. Are there waves in the middle of the ocean?
3. The sea never freezes: true or false?

....

Answers – see page 32.

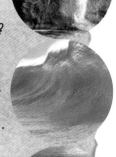

In deep water

- The saltiest sea is the Red Sea.
- There are 50 million billion tonnes of salt in the oceans.
- The biggest ocean is the Pacific, covering one–third of the world.
- The oceans are 3,800 metres deep, on average.
- Mount Everest is the highest mountain at 8,863 metres. But Mauna Kea on Hawaii is taller. Only 4,205 metres is visible – 6,000 metres below the sea makes it 10,205 metres high!

INTERNET LINK

Great virtual trip under the ocean
http://www.seasky.org/mainmenu.html
Learn about the deepest, widest, biggest ocean
pao.cnmoc.navy.mil/educate/neptune/neptune.htm

Why are clouds fluffy or flat?

Clouds are made of tiny drops of water or ice in many different shapes and sizes. The two main kinds are flat stratus clouds and fluffy cumulus clouds. Cumulus are made from the moisture in air billowing upwards. Stratus are flat because they form when a layer of air cools down enough to give up its moisture.

▲ Hailstones are a bit like onions as they are built up in layers. They form when water freezes around ice crystals. When they are heavy enough they fall from clouds as small lumps of ice.

◄ For a smooth flight, airliners must climb high above the clouds and the weather to still dry air.

⮪ Why did the thunder clap?

When you rub a balloon on a jumper you can often feel a tingle. This tingle is static electricity. Inside thunder clouds, strong winds bash ice particles around violently until the cloud gets filled with massive amounts of static electricity. It is this electricity that creates flashes of lightning. As lightning streaks through the air, it heats the air so quickly that the air expands and bangs like a giant balloon bursting. This is a thunder clap.

cirrus cloud

QUICK QUIZ

1. Is a downpour heavier than drizzle?

2. Does lightning come before thunder or after?

3. The safest place to stand in a thunderstorm is under a lone tree: true or false?

....

Answers – see page 32.

altocumulus cloud

altostratus cloud

↗ Why are some clouds like horses' tails?

Not all clouds are made of water drops. Where the air is very cold, high up in the sky, they are made of tiny ice crystals. Ice clouds are very thin and wispy. Sometimes, strong winds blow them out into shapes that look like horses' tails. Clouds like this are called cirrus clouds.

Make your own lightning

You will need:
polythene bag, tape, sticky tack, biscuit tin lids, metal spoon

1. Tape a sheet of polythene (such as a thick waste bag) as flat as you can to a table or chopping board.

2. Stick a big lump of sticky tack to the middle of the inside of a biscuit tin lid.

3. In a darkened room, hold the sticky tack and rub the tin lid vigorously over the polythene sheet for a minute or so.

4. Now bring a second lid or metal spoon within 5 millimetres of the edge of the first lid. You should see a tiny spark of electricity.

cumulus cloud

nimbostratus cloud

stratus cloud

23

When does wind twist?

Tornadoes are small twisting tubes of wind that hang down from thunderclouds like an elephant's trunk. Winds spiral round them at over 300 kilometres an hour, and low pressure in the middle makes them suck things up like giant vacuum cleaners. Tornadoes sweep past in less than 15 minutes, but in this short time they wreak havoc, tossing people, cars, animals and even buildings high in the air like toys.

ⓥ When does it rain blood?

All through history people have told stories of rains of blood falling from the sky. In July 1968, blood-red rain fell on southern England. After the rain, everything was coated in red gritty dust. Scientists realised that the rain was coloured by fine red sand blown thousands of kilometres from the Sahara Desert.

◄ *Most tornadoes form over land. Occasionally they start over the sea, sucking up water to form a waterspout.*

Gale force

- The world's windiest place is George V Island in Antarctica. Winds can blow at over 320 kilometres an hour!
- The Great Hurricane in 1780 killed 22,000 people in the Caribbean.
- The highest ever recorded wind speed was 371 kilometres an hour on Mount Washington in New Hampshire in 1934.
- In 1997 an unverified wind speed of 377 kilometres an hour was recorded in Guam in the Pacific.

⬆ Which winds have eyes?

Hurricanes are giant circular storms that sweep across the oceans and batter the land. Most of the storm is a huge ring of strong winds, dark clouds and torrential rain. But right at the centre of the storm is a small calm area called the eye. A hurricane is sometimes called a typhoon or a cyclone.

QUICK QUIZ

1. Rearrange these in order of strength: gale, breeze, hurricane.
2. Has it ever rained toads?
3. Has a tornado ever sucked a river dry?

....

Answers –
see page 32.

INTERNET LINK

Fun projects about tornadoes and lightning
http://www.ucar.edu/40th/webweather/

Find out more about the very worst weather
http://skydiary.com/kids/tornadoes.html

 # Why is the desert deserted?

Deserts are very dry places where it hardly ever rains. Some deserts are hot, like the Sahara in Africa. Some are very cold, like Antarctica. In hot deserts, what rain there is evaporates so quickly there is little water available for plants.

▲ *Not all deserts are hot and sandy. Some areas near the North and South Poles are ice deserts.*

saguaro cactus

◄ *The saguaro cactus is only found in the foothills and deserts of the United States and Mexico.*

woodpecker

jack rabbit

fennec fox

western fence lizard

⬀ Why is the ground crazy?

Water evaporates quickly in hot deserts. Even whole lakes can dry up entirely. As the water evaporates, it leaves behind a hard crust of minerals in some places, or a crazy-paving pattern of cracked mud in another.

Deserted place

- The world's largest desert is an ice desert – Antarctica.
- The Atacama Desert in Chile usually gets no rain for decades.
- One-fifth of the world's surface is covered by deserts.
- The world's highest recorded temperature of 58°C was in the Sahara Desert, Libya, in 1922.

⬋ Where is the world's biggest sandpit?

Many hot deserts have large areas where there is nothing but sand stretching into the distance. These vast sand seas are called ergs. The biggest is the Rub al Khali in the Arabian peninsula, which covers a total area that is larger than France.

prickly pear

QUICK QUIZ

1. All deserts are sandy: true or false?
2. How much of the world's land is covered by deserts?
3. How do camels survive in the desert for long periods without food?

....

Answers –
see page 32.

INTERNET LINK
Great kids' site introducing deserts
http://desertusa.com
Learn all about deserts
http://mbgnet.mobot.org/sets/desert/

rattlesnake

What rocks hang tight?

Hanging from the roofs of limestone caverns there are often strange, icicle-like formations called stalactites, formed by water dripping from the ceiling. As the water trickles down through the limestone rock above, it dissolves some of the rock. Then as the water drips from the cavern roof, it leaves the dissolved lime behind. Over thousands of years, this lime deposit creates hanging stalactites. It can drip onto the floor, too, and build up pillars called stalagmites.

▸ *The world's longest cave network, Mammoth Cave in Kentucky, was formed by water dissolving limestone rock underground.*

▲ *Limestone caves are turned into natural cathedrals by stalactites and stalagmites.*

⬆ What are the world's biggest holes?

The world's biggest holes are caves. The world's largest single cave is the Sarawak Chamber in Gunung Mulu in Malaysia, which is part of a network of linked caves. The Sarawak Chamber is big enough to hold the world's biggest sports stadium three times over. The world's longest cave network is the Mammoth Cave in Kentucky, which is an amazing 563 kilometres long.

INTERNET LINK
Explore a cave online
http://www.goodearthgraphics.com/virtcave/index.html
All about the world's largest cave system
http://www.nps.gov/maca/home.htm

Making stalactites
You will need:
two jars, washing soda, paper clips, saucer, length of wool

1. Fill two jars with very warm water. Then add washing soda to each, stirring it in until no more will dissolve.

2. Tie a paper clip to each end of a length of wool and lower one into each jar as shown.

3. Set a saucer in between to catch the drips.

4. Leave for 2 or 3 days and you will see your stalactites grow.

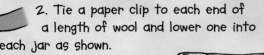

QUICK QUIZ
1. What is a person who knows a lot about caves called?
2. Caves were the world's first art galleries: true or false?
3. Which is bigger — a cave or a cavern?
....
Answers — see page 32.

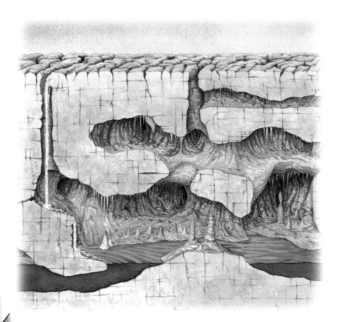

⬆ What makes rocks dissolve?

The world's most spectacular caves, called caverns, are in limestone rock. Streams and rainwater dissolve carbon dioxide gas from the air and turn it into a weak acid. The acid water trickles down through cracks in limestone and gradually dissolves away the rock. As more rock around the crack is dissolved a cavern opens up.

Why are rainforests vanishing?

Rainforests grow in the tropics where there is plenty of rain to keep them watered and sunshine to help them grow. More kinds of animals and plants live here than in all the other places on Earth put together. Large areas of the rainforests have been cleared for agriculture. Vast areas have also been cut down for valuable timber.

emerald
tree boa

toucan

parrot

harpy eagle

sloth

spider
monkey

hummi
bird

jaguar

anaconda

poison
arrow frog

grey tegu
lizard

⊕ Why is the taiga green?

Taiga is a Russian word for the vast, dark green forests that grow over areas of Canada, northern Europe and Siberia. It is very cold in these forests – snow falls thickly in autumn and does not melt until spring. So the only trees that can grow here are evergreen trees, pines and larches. These trees can survive on little water during the frozen winter. They are also cone-shaped to shed snow easily.

QUICK QUIZ

1. What colour are the leaves of deciduous trees in autumn?
2. What kind of tree has thin, needle-like leaves?
3. Where is the world's biggest rainforest?

....

Answers – see page 32.

INTERNET LINK

A good kids' site about habitats
http://enchantedlearning.com/biomes/
Learn more about rainforests at
http://mbgnet.mobot.org/sets/rforest/

⊕ Where do trees undress for winter?

Much of Europe and the USA lies between the warm tropics and the cool regions where taiga grows. Summers are warm, but winters can be so cold that the ground is frozen, and trees cannot get water. So many trees here are deciduous. They shed their leaves in autumn to save water in the winter, then grow new leaves in spring to make the most of the summer warmth.

spring   summer   autumn   winter

Index

Alaska 13, 19
Andes Mountains 9, 15
Antarctica **16**, 25, 26, 27
Appalachian Mountains 9
Arctic Ocean **17**
Asia 8, 11
Atacama Desert, Chile 27
Atlantic Ocean 25

bathyscape 20, 20
beaches 19, *19*

carbon dioxide 29
Caribbean 25
caves 18, **28**, *28*, **29**, 29
China 13
Chyulu Mountains, Kenya 9
cirrus clouds 23
cliffs *18*, 19, *19*
clouds 14, *14*, **22**, 22, **23**, 23, 25
coasts **19**, *19*, 20
comets 4
core **4**, *4*
crust **4**, *4*, 5, 9
cumulus clouds 22, 23

deserts **16**, **26**, *26*, **27**, 27

earthquakes 7, **12**, *12*, 13, *13*
Equator 5
ergs 27, *27*
estuary 19
evaporation 14, *14*, 26, 27

fold mountains 9, *9*
forests 30, **31**

George V Island, Antarctica 25
geyser **11**, *11*
Giant's Causeway, Ireland 6
glaciers **17**, *17*
Great Eastern Erg, Algeria 27
groynes 19, *19*
guyots 21

hailstones 22
Hillary, Edmund 8

Himalaya Mountains, Asia **8**, 9
hurricanes **25**, 25

ice 16, *16*, 17, 22, *22*, 23
igneous rocks **6**, 7
iron 4, 5

lava 6, *6*, 10, *10*
life 4
lightning 22, *22*, 23, *23*
limestone rock 7, 28, *28*, 29, *29*

magma **6**, 7, 10, *10*, 11
Mammoth Cave, Kentucky 28, 29
mantle **4**, *4*
marble **7**
Mariana Trench 20
Mars 4
Mauna Kea, Hawaii 21
metamorphic rock **7**
meteorites **5**, *5*
minerals 27

Moon 19, *19*
Mount Everest, Asia **8**, *8*, 9, 21
Mount St. Helens, North America 11
Mount Washington, New Hampshire 25
mountains **8**, **9**, *9*, 10, 17
mud 7, 27, *27*

Niagara Falls, North America 15
Norgay, Tenzing 8
North America 11, 15
North Pole 17, 26

oceans
  crust 5
  floor **20**, 21
  formation **4**
  tides 19,
  waves 18

Pacific Ocean
  biggest ocean 21
  Mariana Trench 20

record-breaking wave 19
Ring of Fire 11
  wind 25
plates 5, 8, 9
polar ice 17
poles 9

rain
  deserts 26
  geysers 11
  hurricanes 25
  rainforests 30
  tornadoes 24
  water cycle 14, *14*, 15
rainforests **30**, *30*
Red Sea 21
Ring of Fire **11**, *11*
River Amazon, South America 15
River Nile, Africa 15
rivers 14, *14*, **15**, 15
rock **4**, 5
  caves 28, 29
  coasts 19
  earthquakes 12
  igneous **6**
  metamorphic 7
  meteorites 5, *5*
  mountains 9
  sedimentary 7
  volcanoes 10, 11

Sahara Desert, Africa 24, 26, 27
salty sea 21
San Francisco earthquake 13
sand 7, 19, 24, 27, *27*
Sarawak Chamber, Malaysia 29
sea
  ice sheet 17
  tides 19
  tornadoes 25
  water cycle 14, *14*, 15
  waves 18
sea bed 7, **20**
seamounts 21, *21*
sedimentary rocks 7, *7*
shore 13, 18

snow
  Antarctica 16
  comets 4
  mountains 9, *9*, 17
  taiga 31
sonar 20, *20*
South Pole 26
stacks *18*, 19
stalactites **28**, *28*, 29
stalagmites **28**, *28*
static electricity 22
storms 25
stratus clouds 22, 23
Sun 19, *19*

taiga forests 31, *31*
tectonic plates **5**, 9, 12
thunder clouds **22**, 24
tides **19**, *19*
tornadoes **24**, 25
trees 30, 31, *31*
Trieste 20, *20*
tropics 9, 31
tsunami **13**, *13*, 19

valleys 17, 19, 20
Victoria Falls, Zimbabwe 15
volcanoes 6, 9, **10**, *10*, **11**, *11*, 21

water **4**, 5
  caves 28, *28*, 29
  clouds 22, *22*
  desert 16, 26, 27
  geysers 11
  rivers 15
  tornadoes 25
  waves 13, 18, *18*
water cycle 14, *14*
waterfalls **15**, *15*
waves 13, **18**, *18*, 19
weather 7, 22
winds 9, 22, 23, 24, 25

Quick Quiz answers

Page 5
1. 23 hrs 56 mins 4 secs
2. The Pacific
3. Mars and Venus

Page 9
1. Mount McKinley
2. Asia
3. Yes

Page 13
1. False, but it was shaken by the earthquake that destroyed the Portuguese capital Lisbon that year
2. 1906
3. Up to 970 kilometres an hour

Page 17
1. Yes
2. Yes
3. Roald Amundsen

Page 21
1. Atlantic
2. Yes

3. False - the Arctic ocean, for instance, freezes over every year

Page 23
1. Yes
2. Before
3. False – lightning tends to strike prominent places like lone trees

Page 25
1. Breeze, gale, hurricane
2. True - in the village of Acle in Norfolk
3. Yes

Page 27
1. False
2. One-fifth
3. They store reserves of fat in their humps

Page 29
1. Speleologist
2. True
3. A cavern

Page 31
1. Red, yellow and brown
2. A conifer
3. The Amazon Basin, South America